# Diwali

A Buddy Book
by
Julie Murray

## VISIT US AT
### www.abdopublishing.com

Published by ABDO Publishing Company, PO Box 398166, Minneapolis, Minnesota 55439.

Copyright © 2014 by Abdo Consulting Group, Inc. International copyrights reserved in all countries. No part of this book may be reproduced in any form without written permission from the publisher. Buddy Books™ is a trademark and logo of ABDO Publishing Company.

Printed in the United States of America, North Mankato, Minnesota.
092013
012014

PRINTED ON RECYCLED PAPER

Coordinating Series Editor: Rochelle Baltzer
Editor: Sarah Tieck
Contributing Editors: Megan M. Gunderson, Bridget O'Brien, Marcia Zappa
Graphic Design: Denise Esner
Cover Photograph: *Getty Images*: Raj K Raj/Hindustan Times via Getty Images.
Interior Photographs/Illustrations: *Alamy*: DC Premiumstock (p. 21); *AP Photo*: Aman Sharma, File (p. 5), Ajit Solanki (p. 22); *Getty Images*: Bridgeman Art Library (p. 13), Education Images/UIG via Getty Images (p. 11), Jupiterimages (p. 19); *Glow Images*: Sally Ellis (p. 15), photosindia.com (p. 17), Frédéric SOREAU (p. 9); *Shutterstock*: Pikoso.kz (p. 7), JeremyRichards (p. 7), saiko3p (p. 7).

### Library of Congress Cataloging-in-Publication Data

Murray, Julie, 1969-
  Diwali / Julie Murray.
    pages cm. -- (Holidays)
  ISBN 978-1-62403-183-0
  1. Divali--Juvenile literature. I. Title.
  BL1239.82.D58M87 2014
  294.5'36--dc23
                        2013026908

# Table of Contents

# What Is Diwali?

Diwali (dih-VAH-lee) is a Hindu festival. Many people call it the Festival of Lights. This popular festival lasts five days in October or November.

Hindus around the world **celebrate** Diwali. Non-Hindus throughout India also honor this holiday. People decorate their homes, give each other gifts, and light oil lamps.

People gather to watch fireworks during Diwali.

# Around the World

India is a country in southern Asia. It has the highest population of any country except China. India is known for its food, films, and music.

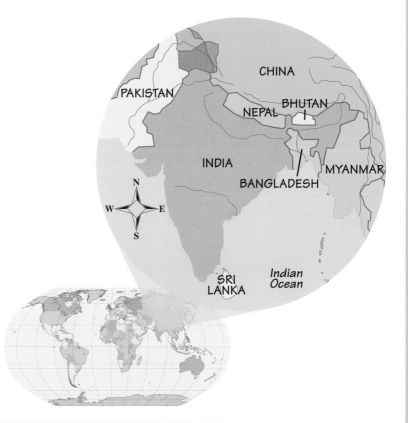

Many Indian women wear colorful saris, which are made of long pieces of fabric.

The Taj Mahal is a famous building in India. An Indian ruler had it built in the 1600s to honor his wife.

India is known for spices such as cumin, mustard seeds, and red pepper. They turn food bright colors and can make it spicy!

# A Popular Faith

Most Indian people practice Hinduism (HIHN-doo-ih-zuhm). Hindus have **sacred** texts and animals. They visit temples and other special places to honor their religion.

The Hindu temple in Tirupati is one of the most visited temples in India.

Hindus believe in many different gods and goddesses. Lakshmi is important during Diwali. Lakshmi is the goddess of wealth. She is known for her beauty. She is often seen sitting or standing on a lotus flower.

# The Story of Diwali

Many historians believe Diwali began as a way to honor the last **harvest** before winter. Indian farmers would seek Lakshmi's blessing on their crops. They prayed for success in the year to come.

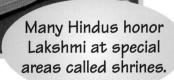

Many Hindus honor Lakshmi at special areas called shrines.

Diwali also honors the god Rama. Rama is the hero of an ancient Indian poem called the *Ramayana*.

In the poem, Rama is forced to leave his home. He returns after 14 years. His return is **celebrated** during Diwali.

Rama is one of the most commonly worshipped Hindu gods.

# Row of Lights

Diwali gets its name from the rows of oil lamps that are lit during the festival. Diwali comes from the Sanskrit word *dipavali,* which means "row of lights." These lamps stand for inner light and knowledge.

Some people believe that Lakshmi searches for welcoming homes. So, families light lamps to invite her in. The Diwali lamps are also lit to welcome Rama.

The oil lamps are called *diyas*.

# During Diwali

People do special activities for Diwali. They may clean and decorate their homes or wear new clothes. Some people give each other gifts. Many watch fireworks.

A new business year starts during Diwali. So, it is a time when many people pray for success.

Presents are a fun part of Diwali.

# Diwali Dishes

During Diwali, people may give each other the gift of food. They often give sweets or dried fruits. Many families gather to share meals.

People serve their favorite sweets during Diwali. Sometimes, nuts and spices are added.

# Diwali Today

Diwali is considered a national holiday in India. It is a Hindu holiday during which people **worship**. They also decorate their homes, eat special meals with family, and pray for blessings. It is a time to **celebrate**!

Fireworks, clay lamps, bonfires, and lights are everywhere during Diwali!

# Rangoli

During Diwali, people decorate their floors with *rangoli*. These patterns may be drawn or made out of beads or flowers.

One popular shape during Diwali is the lotus flower. Rangoli helps welcome Lakshmi into people's homes.

Rangoli is colorful!

# Important Words

**celebrate**  to observe a holiday with special events.

**harvest**  the gathering of a crop.

**sacred**  (SAY-kruhd)  connected with worship of a god.

**worship**  to honor a god by praying or through other acts.

# Web Sites

**To learn more about Diwali,**
visit ABDO Publishing Company online. Web sites about Diwali are featured on our Book Links page. These links are routinely monitored and updated to provide the most current information available.

**www.abdopublishing.com**

# Index